London

i-SPY

INTRODUCTION

London is one of the greatest cities in the world. Its long history and endless variety make it a fascinating city to explore. Evidence of London's past is all around – and is easy to spot. There are sections of Roman settlement still visible in the city dating back 2000 years; the Tower of London dates back 1000 years to William the Conqueror; Sir Christopher Wren's masterpiece, St Paul's Cathedral, dates from the 17th century; the London Eye and the Shard are recent additions to the skyline and form part of the modern landscape of the ever-changing city. It has too much history and is too large for anyone to know it all but, with i-SPY London, you can get to know it very well – and go on to discover more things for yourself.

There are so many places to see and explore and the best way to explore London is on foot. The Underground also means you can move about London easily for variety, perhaps seeing the East End in the morning and Buckingham Palace in the afternoon. Buses are interesting too, as are the launches on the Thames and Regent's Canal. For outer London, trains are usually the best way to travel. But before you set off on your journey of exploration, take a look at the Iconic London section at the end of this book – it contains i-SPIES for you to spot all around the city, which will help you collect points as you go.

How to use your i-SPY book

The book is arranged by area to help you get the best out of your visit. As you explore, don't forget to tick off the sights as you see them. You need 1000 points to send off for your i-SPY certificate (see page 64) but that is not too difficult because there are masses of points in every book. Each entry has a star or circle and points value beside it. The stars represent harder to spot entries. As you make each i-SPY, write your score in the circle or star. Where there is a question, double your score if you can answer it. Check your answers on page 63.

Points: 10

SHERLOCK HOLMES MUSEUM

The interior of 221b Baker Street, which was the fictional address of the great detective, has been faithfully created exactly as described in the published stories.

LONDON ZOO

Points: 10

London Zoo, in Regent's Park, is one of the world's most famous zoos and is home to over 18,000 animals. There is a programme of daily talks, giving visitors the opportunity to learn more about the animals from their keepers.

MADAME TUSSAUDS

Points: 10

Madame Tussauds London

This museum of waxworks is a major London attraction, where the lack of ropes or barriers allows for real close-up photo opportunities with the rich and famous! The models are regularly updated, so you are just as likely to see the latest Oscar winner alongside a member of the Royal Family.

Points: 20

BBC BROADCASTING HOUSE

BasPhoto / Shutterstock.com

Located on Portland Place, this is the central London headquarters of the BBC's news, radio, television and online services. The original 1930s building shown here has had a modern extension that was officially opened in 2013. The building incorporates a memorial called 'Breathing' which commemorates journalists who have been killed while carrying out their work around the world.

Points: 15

Harley Street has been associated with medicine since the middle of the 19th century, when doctors were attracted to the large Georgian houses and their proximity to main line train stations. There are now over 3000 people employed in the private clinics and practices in the area.

REGENT'S PARK

Points: 10

Cedric Weber / Shutterstock.com

One of the Royal Parks of London and a lovely place to stroll or have a picnic. Look out for some of the wild birds that live here too – there are more than 100 different species.

OXFORD STREET

Points: 5

Oxford Street is one of the most famous shopping streets in the world. Always busy, take a look at the modern crossing at the junction with Regent Street.

Points: 10

SELFRIDGES

First opened in 1909, Selfridges department store dominates the west end of Oxford Street. The clock above the entrance is known as 'The Queen of Time' and was added in 1931.

THE WALLACE COLLECTION

Points: 20

This art collection includes masterpieces by Titian, Rubens, Reynolds, Van Dyke and Canaletto, displayed in rooms that are filled with fine furniture and porcelain.

Points: 10

MARBLE ARCH

Marble Arch, designed in 1827 by John Nash, is made of carrara marble – a high-quality whitish-grey marble. It was originally built as the entrance to Buckingham Palace, but it was moved to its current location, at the north-east corner of Hyde Park, in 1851.

THE SERPENTINE LAKE

Points: 15

Peace and serenity is never very far away in London. In Hyde Park, you can take a rowing boat out on this man-made lake and admire the views, or even go for a swim in the lido area in the summer.

Points: 10

HYDE PARK

A public park since early in the 17th century, Hyde Park is one of London's most prized open spaces. It has hosted many major music festivals.

PRINCESS DIANA MEMORIAL FOUNTAIN

Points: 15

Sandor Gora / Shutterstock.com

Located in the south-west corner of Hyde Park, this is not a fountain in the traditional sense, but a large, oval stream bed about 50 x 80m (164 x 262ft).

Points: 10

SPEAKERS' CORNER

Located at the north-east side of Hyde Park, Speakers' Corner is a space for orators and hecklers to debate the issues of the day.

PETER PAN STATUE

Points: 15

J.M. Barrie, author of the Peter Pan stories, lived near Kensington Gardens. These gardens inspired some of his work, and the boy who never grew up is immortalised in a bronze statue there. Look out too for the squirrels, rabbits, mice and fairies climbing the statue's plinth.

Points: 15

ALBERT MEMORIAL

Gleaming in gold leaf following a major restoration project, the Albert Memorial in Kensington Gardens is dedicated to Queen Victoria's husband, who died in 1861.

ROYAL ALBERT HALL

Points: 15

A major arts venue hosting classical music (including the world famous Proms), rock concerts, ballet, tennis and award ceremonies. It is one of the most atmospheric music venues in the world.

Points: 10

HARRODS

Perhaps the most famous shop in the world, it boasts a huge array of products. The food hall on the ground floor houses a vast selection of foodstuffs from the exotic to the everyday. Make sure you allocate plenty of time to visit!

HARVEY NICHOLS

Points: 10

This is another iconic Kensington store. It started out as a small linen shop in 1831 and now has six floors of fashion and food, including a restaurant on the fifth floor.

VICTORIA AND ALBERT MUSEUM

Points: 15

Referred to as the V&A, this fine museum is housed on four floors. Endless galleries display fine and applied art collections, sculpture, furniture, fashion and photographs.

Points: 15

SCIENCE MUSEUM

chrisdorney / Shutterstock.com

This vast collection includes Stevenson's Rocket and the Apollo 10 command module, as well as interactive displays, flight simulators and an IMAX cinema.

NATURAL HISTORY MUSEUM

Points: 15

This vast museum contains hundreds of exciting interactive exhibits with sections on dinosaurs, ecology and the animal world.

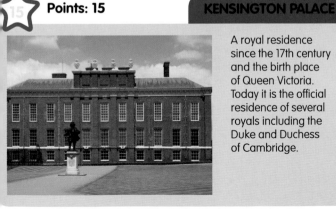

Points: 15

KENSINGTON PALACE

A royal residence since the 17th century and the birth place of Queen Victoria. Today it is the official residence of several royals including the Duke and Duchess of Cambridge.

ST JAMES'S PARK

Points: 10

Once one of Henry VIII's many hunting grounds, this is the oldest of London's royal parks. It is the setting for many royal ceremonies, and also has some resident pelicans which you can watch being fed every afternoon.

Points: 15

ST JAMES'S PALACE

Dating back to the first half of the 16th century, this building was designed as a royal residence. Occupied by high-ranking Crown servants since 1922, Queen Elizabeth II made her first speech as Queen here.

FLORENCE NIGHTINGALE STATUE

Points: 15

This statue of the 'Lady with the Lamp' stands in front of the memorial to the Crimean War, in which she famously nursed the wounded soldiers. They are located just off The Mall.

Points: 10

GREEN PARK

Green Park opened to the public in 1826 and today is a popular open space for early-morning joggers and walkers. Royal gun salutes are fired from this park to mark certain occasions throughout the year.

THE RITZ

Points: 15

This is one of the most famous hotels in London. The experience of afternoon tea may be a little formal so pop into the foyer instead and see where the rich and famous stay.

Points: 10

EROS

The statue of Eros, the Greek god of love, is located in Piccadilly Circus. It is believed to be the first in the world to be cast in aluminium, and though it was originally designed to depict Eros's twin brother, Anteros, the people of London have always known it as Eros.

FORTNUM AND MASON

Points: 15

Fortnum's first opened in 1707 and continues to be world famous for its high-quality goods. It was the first store in the world to sell Heinz baked beans – in 1886!

Points: 20

BEADLES AT BURLINGTON ARCADE

The Beadles are a private police force located in the Burlington Arcade. They have been guarding the shops there since 1819 and can be identified by their Edwardian frock coats and top hats.

BOND STREET

Points: 10

The two halves of this road, known as 'Old' and 'New' Bond Street, have been home to many upmarket boutiques and jewellers since the street became a fashionable place to live in the 18th century.

Points: 15

ROYAL ACADEMY OF ARTS

This art institution in Burlington House stages big, thematic shows and is famous for its summer exhibition.

PICCADILLY CIRCUS

Points: 10 16

Located at the junction of Piccadilly and Regent Street, Piccadilly Circus has long been a focal point in central London, famous for its neon advertising signs and home to the statue of Eros. It is particularly colourful at night.

ADMIRALTY ARCH

Points: 15

This is a large building located between The Mall and Trafalgar Square. As the name suggests, traffic and pedestrians pass through an arch incorporated into the building.

Points: 15

CHANGING OF THE GUARD

A magnificent ceremony that takes place outside Buckingham Palace every day in the summer and every other day in winter. Take up a good viewpoint for some wonderful photographs!

Thomas Barrat / Shutterstock.com

HORSE GUARDS PARADE

Points: 15

Originally Henry VIII's tournament ground, there are ceremonies involving the mounted guard that take place here twice a day.

Jaroslaw Grudzinski / Shutterstock.com

Points: 10

BUCKINGHAM PALACE

The Queen's official residence has over 600 rooms and boasts a 42-acre garden. The palace's state apartments are open to the public in summer; tours include the Throne Room, the Picture Gallery and the State Dining Room. If the Royal Standard is flying overhead, the Queen is in residence. Standing in front of the Palace is the Victoria Monument which is a memorial to Queen Victoria who reigned from 1837 until her death in 1901. As well as the statue of Victoria herself, the memorial also incorporates statues representing constancy, courage, victory, charity, truth and motherhood.

THE MALL

Points: 10

The Mall is famous the world over as 'The Red Road'. It runs from Buckingham Palace to Admiralty Arch.

Points: 20

SHEPHERD MARKET

Tucked away, this square in Mayfair is surrounded by lanes full of cafes, small shops and restaurants. The square is named after Edward Shepherd, who worked on its development between 1735 and 1746.

BERKELEY SQUARE

Points: 15

This large, rectangular open space was made famous by the song 'A Nightingale Sang in Berkeley Square'. London has many such squares where you can take a break and rest your feet.

Ron Ellis / Shutterstock.com

Points: 20

CLARENCE HOUSE

Named after its first resident, William, Duke of Clarence, this house was designed by John Nash and dates from 1827. It is now the official residence of The Prince of Wales and the Duchess of Cornwall.

Padmayogini / Shutterstock.com

REGENT STREET

Points: 10

One of the most famous streets in London, Regent Street is well known for its Christmas lights, usually switched on by a celebrity in November.

Points: 15

HAMLEYS

A 'must-visit' for children, this fantastic Regent Street toy store is housed over seven floors and packed with every type of toy and game imaginable.

LIBERTY

Points: 20

Built in 1924, this mock-Tudor department store on Regent Street is a treasure-trove of fashion, cosmetics, ceramics and printed fabrics.

LONDON PALLADIUM

Points: 20

Tucked away in Argyll Street, off Oxford Street, the London Palladium is probably the most famous theatre in the UK and is the venue for many blockbuster productions.

Points: 15

CARNABY STREET

The heartbeat of 'Swinging London' in the 1960s may have lost some of its original charm but it is still a fashionable shopping street.

LEICESTER SQUARE

Points: 10
Double points if you spot someone famous

Lined with cinemas, this square is the scene of frequent celebrity-studded film premières. In the centre of the square, you'll find Leicester Square Gardens, where you can see a statue of William Shakespeare (shown in the photo).

TRAFALGAR SQUARE

Points: 10

10

This square is dominated by the facade of the National Gallery as well as the 50m (165ft) column dedicated to Admiral Lord Nelson. The base is guarded by four massive lions – fortunately they are made out of bronze!

15 **Points: 15**

NATIONAL GALLERY

This neo-classical style gallery has a superb collection of European paintings dating from 1250 to 1900. The collection includes works by Botticelli, Leonardo da Vinci, Rembrandt, Gainsborough, Turner, Cezanne and Van Gogh.

NATIONAL PORTRAIT GALLERY

Points: 15

Visit this collection to see history through art – portraits and representations of important figures throughout the ages, including English monarchs since medieval times.

ST MARTIN-IN-THE-FIELDS

Situated at the corner of Trafalgar Square, this lovely 18th-century building is the parish church of the Royal Family. There has been a church on this site for about 800 years. Originally it was surrounded by fields, which is how it got its name.

Points: 15

CHARLES I STATUE

This statue of King Charles I on the south side of Trafalgar Square stands at the point from which all distances to London are measured on road signs around the country. Look out for the plaque on the ground just behind it.

Points: 15

CHINATOWN

Points: 10

10

Best seen in the evening, the area around Gerrard Street is home to a vibrant Chinese community with lots of restaurants, supermarkets and souvenir shops.

10

Points: 10

WEST END THEATRE

London's Theatreland is one of the largest theatre districts in the world, with many world famous shows. The theatres are mainly concentrated around Leicester Square, Shaftesbury Avenue and The Strand.

Points: 15

MUSEUM OF LONDON

Located on London Wall, this extensive collection depicts the history of London, with excellent Roman artefacts from nearby excavations and superb displays on all periods.

FROST FAIR MURAL

Top Spot!   **Points: 25**

Before the building of modern bridges, the River Thames often froze in winter. Underneath Southwark Bridge is a mural of the famous Frost Fair of 1564.

Points: 15

ROYAL COURTS OF JUSTICE

These buildings, built in the Victorian Gothic style, handle many of the nation's major civil court cases. They are located on The Strand.

GUILDHALL

Points: 15

Guildhall, off Gresham Street, has been the administrative centre of the City of London for almost 900 years. The current building was begun in 1411 and includes a medieval great hall, which is still used for ceremonies and banquets.

Points: 15

OLD BAILEY

This is the Central Criminal Court of England and Wales. The gold statue on the top is of Lady Justice, who holds a sword in one hand and scales of justice in the other.

Points: 20

LINCOLN'S INN FIELDS

Lincoln's Inn Fields is the largest public square in London. The chambers of many law firms surround the green area.

SIR JOHN SOANE'S MUSEUM

Top Spot!   **Points: 25**

Overlooking Lincoln's Inn Fields, this house contains the private collection of the architect who died in 1837. It includes famous artworks, furniture and artefacts, such as an Egyptian sarcophagus.

Points: 20

BANK OF ENGLAND

The Bank of England is one of the oldest banks in the world and the issuer of all bank notes for England and Wales. Located at the rear of the building is a museum which traces the history of the bank from 1694 to the present day.

TOWER BRIDGE

Points: 10

Tower Bridge has stood over the River Thames since 1894 and is one of the finest, most recognisable landmarks in the world.

Points: 15

HMS BELFAST

GTS Productions / Shutterstock.com

A World War II cruiser, with nine decks to explore – everything from the Captain's bridge to the massive boiler and engine rooms. It is moored off the south bank of the River Thames, close to Tower Bridge.

Points: 10
Double with answer

TOWER OF LONDON

Originally built by William the Conqueror, the Tower of London has been a fortress and a prison, as well as a palace. The Beefeaters and famous ravens guard the priceless Crown Jewels.

What is the correct title of the Beefeaters?

Points: 15

BARBICAN

The Barbican is a monolithic cultural centre with an art gallery, cinema, theatre and auditorium. It was opened in 1982 and is an example of the Brutalist style of architecture.

TOWER 42

Tupungato / Shutterstock.com

Located on Old Broad Street, Tower 42 was the first skyscraper to be built in the City and was completed in 1980. Originally known as the NatWest Tower, it was renamed in reference to its 42 floors, by new owners in 1995.

 **Points: 15**

THE GHERKIN

Kiev Victor / Shutterstock.com

Officially its name is 30 St Mary Axe, or sometimes the Swiss Re Building, but most of us know it as the Gherkin!

Points: 10

Points: 10

ST PAUL'S CATHEDRAL

Christopher Wren's most famous monument was completed in 1708. It contains the tombs of Nelson and Wellington and has played host to a number of important royal occasions from Queen Victoria's Diamond Jubilee celebrations in 1897 to the wedding of Prince Charles and Princess Diana in 1981.

MILLENNIUM BRIDGE

Points: 15

The first new bridge across the River Thames since Tower Bridge opened in 1894, and the first ever for pedestrians only. The Millennium Bridge is now an established feature linking St Paul's Cathedral with the Tate Modern.

ST KATHARINE DOCKS

Points: 15

Built in 1828, the docks traded for over 120 years and were closed after larger ships could no longer pass through the lock into the basin. Following World War II damage, the area was redeveloped and given new life.

Points: 20

THE MONUMENT

The Monument stands 60.6m (199ft) high and exactly 60.6m (199ft) from the spot in Pudding Lane where the Great Fire of London started in 1666. It was built shortly afterwards to commemorate the Great Fire and also to celebrate the rebuilding of the city. There are great views from the top if you're willing to climb the 311 steps!

Points: 5

BIG BEN

Probably the most famous landmark in London, Big Ben is actually the nickname of the 14-tonne bell, cast in 1858, of the four-faced clock (the largest in Britain) at the top of the clock tower in the Houses of Parliament.

HOUSES OF PARLIAMENT

Points: 5

This has been the seat of English government since 1512 and is home to both the House of Commons and the House of Lords. This vast mock-gothic palace was built after a fire destroyed the original building in 1834.

Points: 10

DOWNING STREET

This most famous of streets was built by Sir George Downing in 1684. Number 10 has been the official residence of serving British prime ministers since 1735.

OLIVER CROMWELL STATUE

Following the English Civil War, Cromwell took control of the country under the title Lord Protector. In 1649, Cromwell famously abolished Christmas! This statue of him stands outside the Houses of Parliament.

What was Cromwell's nickname?

Points: 20
Double with answer

SIR WINSTON CHURCHILL STATUE

This massive Parliament Square statue was erected in 1973 and depicts the wartime prime minister, Sir Winston Churchill.

Points: 15

Points: 20

RICHARD THE LIONHEART STATUE

King Richard I ruled from 1189–1199 and although he spoke little English and spent very little time in England he remains a much loved ruler. His statue stands outside the House of Lords.

THE CENOTAPH

Points: 10

Built in the 1920s by Sir Edwin Lutyens, this bleak stone memorial commemorates those who died in both World Wars. Wreaths are placed here each year on Remembrance Sunday, which is the closest one to November 11th.

Points: 15

STATUE OF BOUDICCA

The warrior queen of the Iceni tribe rose up against the Romans in AD 61. Her statue stands prominently on the embankment overlooking Westminster Bridge.

WESTMINSTER ABBEY

Points: 10

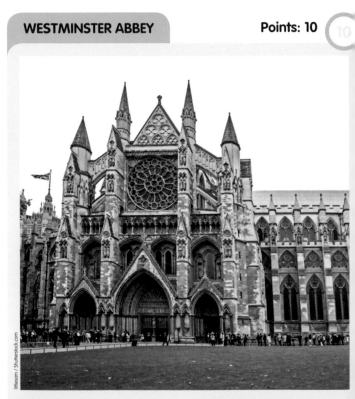

littlesam / Shutterstock.com

This has been a site of worship for over 1000 years and was originally a Benedictine monastery. The 13th-century abbey is the resting place of countless regal, military and literary names. Every monarch since William the Conqueror, except two, has been crowned under its roof.

Points: 15

CABINET WAR ROOMS

Winston Churchill and the British Government directed troops from these basement offices during World War II. The Cabinet War Rooms form part of the Churchill War Rooms museum on King Charles Street.

CLEOPATRA'S NEEDLE

Points: 10

Dating from around 1460 BC, this Egyptian obelisk was brought to London from Alexandria (the royal city of Cleopatra) in 1878 and erected on Victoria Embankment to commemorate British victories in the Battle of the Nile and the Battle of Alexandria. Measuring about 21m (69ft), it is made of red granite and is inscribed with Egyptian hieroglyphs.

Points: 20

BATTLE OF BRITAIN MONUMENT

The monument pays tribute to those who took part in the Battle of Britain, fought in the skies over Britain in World War II. It was unveiled in 2005 and is situated on Victoria Embankment.

SOMERSET HOUSE

Points: 15

A major arts and cultural centre close to the River Thames, in winter the central courtyard is home to an open-air ice rink.

Points: 15
Double with answer

THE SAVOY

Located on the Strand, the Savoy first opened in 1889. It was Britain's first luxury hotel, and to this day it remains one of the world's finest hotels. In 2010, it underwent a major refurbishment – costing £220m!

What is unusual about Savoy Court, the entrance road to the hotel?

5

Points: 5

WHITEHALL

A broad street running from Trafalgar Square to Parliament Square, it is the seat of political power and home to many civil servants.

TATE BRITAIN

Points: 10

10

Built by the 19th-century sugar magnate Henry Tate, this gallery on Millbank houses art from the 16th to the 20th centuries.

LONDON EYE

Points: 5

5

Planned as a temporary exhibit for the millennium celebrations, this giant Ferris wheel has proved to be a firm favourite for visitors of all ages. On a clear day the 360-degree views are stunning.

JuliusKielaitis / Shutterstock.com

10

Points: 10

LONDON AQUARIUM

Housed in County Hall, the London Aquarium hosts 14 different aquatic themed zones, which hold 5000 sea creatures.

Steve Mann / Shutterstock.com

Points: 20

SOUTHWARK CATHEDRAL

There has been a church on this site since 1086 although it did not become a cathedral until 1905. It houses the most interesting collection of tombs and epitaphs outside of Westminster Abbey.

TATE MODERN

Points: 10

This Art Deco former power station is Britain's national museum of modern and contemporary art, displaying major works by Matisse and Picasso as well as exhibitions and installations.

Points: 15

SHAKESPEARE'S GLOBE THEATRE

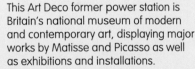

Standing a few hundred metres from the original site, the theatre which presented many of Shakespeare's greatest plays has been lovingly recreated with materials, techniques and craftsmanship of 400 years ago.

OXO TOWER

Points: 15

When the makers of OXO beef stock cubes wanted to advertise their product with large illuminated signs in the 1920s, they were refused permission. The result? Build your own advertising! The tower is now known as OXO Tower Wharf and contains shops, restaurants, galleries and design studios.

Philip Bird LRPS CPAGB / Shutterstock.com

Points: 15

THE SHARD

Towering over the whole of London, this 95-storey building resembles a shard of glass. It was opened in 2013 and contains offices, apartments, restaurants and a hotel, plus an observation deck on the 72nd level.

Points: 25   Top Spot!

CLINK PRISON MUSEUM

Slang now for any prison, 'The Clink' originally referred to the Clink Prison on Clink Street. However, it is now a museum that illustrates the history of the infamous jail that once stood on this site, and of the surrounding area.

IMPERIAL WAR MUSEUM

Points: 20

The Imperial War Museum on Lambeth Road tells the story of British military conflict from World War I to the present day. Among the exhibitions are 'A Family in Wartime' and 'The Holocaust'.

Points: 15

LONDON DUNGEON

The London Dungeon brings the gruesome side of London's history to life with the use of displays, rides and live action. Uncover the truth about the Great Plague, Jack the Ripper and the Great Fire of London at the museum which occupies part of the County Hall building.

BOROUGH MARKET

Points: 20

London's oldest fruit and vegetable market has existed since at least 1276, and has been on the current site in Southwark Street since the mid-18th century. The market now has over 100 stalls and sells all kinds of interesting food from pork pies and chocolate to handmade breakfast cereal.

Points: 20

GOLDEN HINDE

In St Mary Overie Dock, you will find a full-size replica of Sir Francis Drake's galleon in which he circumnavigated the globe between 1577 and 1580.

IMAX

Points: 20

This large-format cinema, close to Waterloo Station, features a screen measuring 20 x 26m (66 x 85ft) – it's the biggest screen in the UK!

Points: 10

COVENT GARDEN

This is London's oldest planned square, built in the 1630s on the site of the Saxon town of Lundenwic. Long associated with its fruit and vegetable market, Covent Garden now has many shops, bars and restaurants.

ROYAL OPERA HOUSE

Points: 15

Located in Covent Garden, the Royal Opera House has its own orchestra and is home to both the Royal Opera and the Royal Ballet.

Points: 15

LONDON TRANSPORT MUSEUM

Travel through time and learn the history of London's transport system, from 1800 to the present day. Most exhibits allow for a close-up inspection of old trams, buses and trains.

BRITISH MUSEUM

Points: 10

Britain's oldest museum opened in 1759. It contains an array of artefacts illustrating the history of human art and culture from around the world, and includes the Rosetta Stone and the Parthenon sculptures. It is located on Great Russell Street.

Dan Breckwoldt / Shutterstock.com

Points: 15

BRITISH LIBRARY

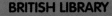

Situated on Euston Road, the national library of the UK is one of the world's largest research libraries. It contains over 150 million items and receives a copy of every book produced in the UK and Ireland (including this one!).

BT TOWER

Points: 5 5

With an overall height of 189m (620ft), this telecommunications tower with its revolving restaurant at the top became one of the capital's top attractions when it opened in 1965. It was closed to the public for security reasons in 1980.

10 **Points: 10**

ST PANCRAS STATION

Renovated in the 2000s at a cost of £800 million, the refurbished station is the terminus for Eurostar™ services to and from continental Europe, as well as serving the East Midlands of England.

BATTERSEA POWER STATION

Points: 10

This famous south bank landmark was designed by Giles Gilbert Scott, who also designed the red telephone box! It was closed in 1983 but is now being redeveloped as apartments, shops and offices.

Points: 15

CUTTY SARK

Launched in 1869 for transporting tea back from China, the Cutty Sark travelled the world and was the fastest clipper of her day. She has been moored up in dry dock in Greenwich since 1957 and offers a fascinating insight into the daily life of the merchant seamen.

Points: 20
Double with answer

CANARY WHARF

Built on the site of the West India Docks, Canary Wharf takes its name from the quay where fruit and vegetables used to arrive from the Canary Islands. It contains three of the UK's tallest buildings.

Do you know their names?

WEMBLEY STADIUM

Points: 15
Double if you see a match here

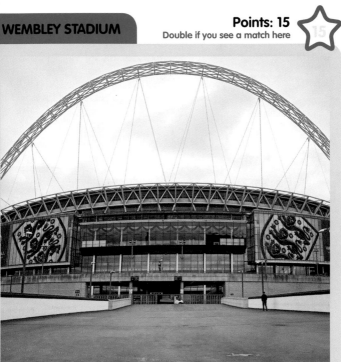

The world's most expensive football stadium, when completed in 2007, was built on the site of the original Wembley Stadium that had stood since 1923. Most England home international matches are played here as well as all major domestic football finals. Wembley is also home from time to time to other sports such as American football and pop concerts where the capacity can reach a quarter of a million people!

REGENT'S CANAL

Points: 20

The canal, now mostly used by pleasure craft, runs from Little Venice near Paddington, through Regent's Park and London Zoo to Camden Town.

Points: 20

NATIONAL MARITIME MUSEUM

The National Maritime Museum in Greenwich displays an unrivalled collection of maritime artefacts including maps, paintings, figureheads and Horatio Nelson's uniform from the Battle of Trafalgar.

O2 ARENA

Points: 20

Originally a temporary structure built for the millennium celebrations, the O2 Arena in Greenwich is now a major indoor venue for concerts and sporting events.

Points: 25   **Top Spot!**

THAMES BARRIER

Built to stop London from flooding, its 10 futuristic gates are supported by seven concrete piers. It has been operational since 1982 and has been closed nearly 200 times since then.

GUARD IN BEARSKIN

Points: 5

Karol Kozlowski / Shutterstock.com

These helmets, traditionally made of real bearskin, are worn by the Foot Guards of the British Army Household Division, who are responsible for guarding the monarch.

Points: 15

DRAGON

Dragon statues stand guard at several boundary points around the City of London. Most of them are smaller replicas of the two on Victoria Embankment, and are holding the shield from the City's coat of arms.

DOUBLE-DECKER BUS

Points: 5

Chris Jenner / Shutterstock.com

London is famous for its red buses and you won't have to wait long before you see one go past. Taking a ride on a double-decker bus is a great way to see the city.

5 Points: 5

You will find newspaper sellers on the streets all around the centre of London.

BLUE PLAQUE

Points: 10 **10**

Over the last 150 years, more than 900 blue plaques have been placed on buildings all over London to mark the famous people who have lived or worked there. How many will you find?

Points: 5

These signs mark the entrances to the stations on the London Underground rail network.

BLACK TAXI

Points: 5

London's official taxis can be seen all over the city. If the yellow sign above the windscreen is illuminated then the taxi is available for hire.

Oliver Hoffmann / Shutterstock.com

56

Points: 5

PHONE BOX

These distinctive red telephone boxes first appeared on the streets of London in 1926 and became widespread around the city, although they are not used as much now as they were in the past.

CHELSEA PENSIONER

Points: 10

With their distinctive scarlet frock coats and black tricorne hats, the Chelsea Pensioners are a familiar sight around the city. These ladies and men are all British Army veterans who live at the Royal Hospital Chelsea.

BUSKER

Points: 5 5

Buskers are people who sing or perform in public places in the hope that passers-by will give them a tip. From bagpipe players to acrobats to living statues, they can be very entertaining.

Stuart Monk / Shutterstock.com

5 **Points: 5**

CYCLE COURIER

Sometimes the quickest way to get around London is by bike, so cycle couriers are often employed to take letters or parcels directly from one place to another. They usually carry their deliveries in a large bag on their back.

ANY LONDON BRIDGE

Points: 5

There are several road bridges that span the River Thames. Many of them have been rebuilt over the years, but of the city centre bridges that are standing today, the oldest is Westminster Bridge, which was built in 1862.

Points: 15

EIIR SIGN

The Queen's cypher with crown above it can be seen in many places and on many uniforms around the city. The E stands for Elizabeth, the II denotes that she is the second English monarch of that name and the R stands for Regina, which is Latin for Queen.

SOUVENIR STALL

Points: 5 5

There are many souvenir stalls around the city where you can buy all sorts of things like T-shirts, keyrings, fridge magnets or ornaments to remind you of your trip to London.

5 **Points: 5**

BEEFEATER

Beefeater is the nickname given to the Yeoman Warders, who guard the Tower of London, and the Yeoman of the Guard, who play a ceremonial role in many royal events. Their distinctive Tudor uniforms are almost identical.

UNION JACK

Points: 5 5

The national flag of the United Kingdom is a familiar sight in London. It incorporates the crosses of the patron saints of England, Scotland and Northern Ireland – the Welsh flag isn't represented because when the Union Jack was first created in 1606, Wales was part of England.

Points: 20

This race is usually held every April and takes the participants on a 26.2 mile tour of the city: through Greenwich, over Tower Bridge to the Docklands, then along the Embankment to end on The Mall. It is a prestigious race to win for a professional athlete, but most of the thousands of runners are there for fun or to raise money for charity.

RIVER BOAT

Points: 5

5

One of the regular boats travelling up and down the Thames is the River Bus. This operates between Putney in the west and Woolwich in the east, and is a good way to see the sights along the river.

5

Points: 5

PUB

The typical London pub is on a street corner and is a place where local people and visitors can have a drink and a chat. Some of London's pubs are hundreds of years old and are ornately decorated inside.

INDEX

i-SPY

How to get your i-SPY certificate and badge

Let us know when you've become a super-spotter with 1000 points and we'll send you a special certificate and badge!

HERE'S WHAT TO DO!

UNDERGROUND

- Ask an adult to check your score.

- Visit www.collins.co.uk/i-SPY to apply for your certificate. If you are under the age of 13 you will need a parent or guardian to do this.

- We'll send your certificate via email and you'll receive a brilliant badge through the post!